MW01519253

She Is Perfect for you

written by Nick DeMann
Illustrated by Mandee Monson

To my Mom, Grandmas, and 'Aussie Grandma.'

Thank you.

Foreword

No matter your family circumstances, there has been a woman somewhere who has loved you like her own. She could be a neighbor, family friend, aunt, grandma, sister, co-worker, or teacher. She blessed your life with divine gifts that God gave her.

In Heaven above live all boys and girls. They live in peace and joy. There, they are nurtured and grow in love. The Father of Heaven and Earth lives there and loves each child dearly. He created a plan of happiness for all to increase their potential even further.

A little boy was with his Creator and was being taught.

"I love you and I am very proud of you," Christ said. "Today is a great day for you. I am excited about your growth on earth. You will do amazing things; things I created you for."

With generosity in Jesus' eyes, He asked, "Tyson, do you have any more questions?"

After some thought, Tyson asked, "Savior, you have taught me so much, thank you. You know I am going to earth soon. I know you will always love me wherever I go. While I am away from you, is there someone who will love me like you on earth?"

"Come, my child, follow me," Christ said. "I will introduce you to someone special."

Tyson and Christ walked off the soft edge of the clouds right into a valley on earth. They went into a beautiful home with two people inside. Inside the home, Christ put his hand on Tyson's shoulder, smiled and said, "Let me show you who she is." When Christ said those words, Tyson saw a beautiful young woman nurturing another older woman. He could see love and dedication in the young woman's eyes. She had God's love shining within her.

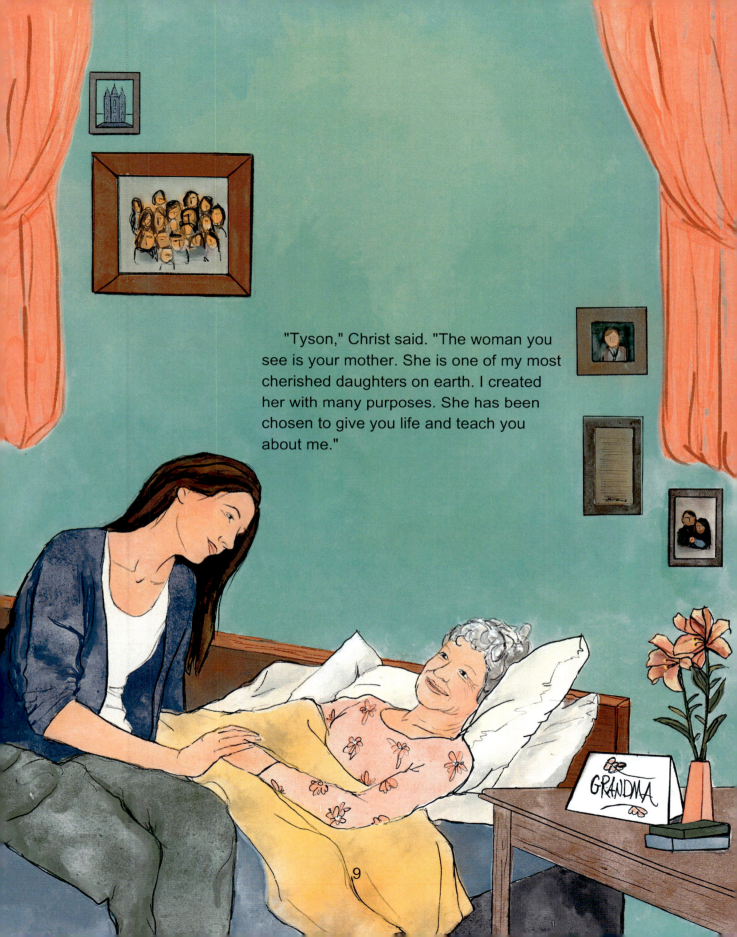

"Tyson," Christ said. "The woman you see is your mother. She is one of my most cherished daughters on earth. I created her with many purposes. She has been chosen to give you life and teach you about me."

GRANDMA

9

As they followed her life, Tyson spoke, "Wow, she is strong and kind. I can tell that she is true and valiant. No matter how big the storm of life is, no matter the difficulty, no matter the struggle and the heartache, she keeps going and never gives up. She is extraordinary."

10

Tyson turned to Christ and asked, "Savior, will you please tell me more about her?"

Christ responded with a heartfelt smile as sincere as a mother holding her newborn baby. "Certainly." With tears in His eyes, He said, "She is going to help you in many ways. I will reveal a few ways to you now."

11

"Your mother is blessed with grace and can give it easily and freely. Grace helps troubled people become better; it is a product of peace. When your mother extends grace, she is giving it from her heart.

12

"Grace helps you to be your best and then go beyond your best. Even when your best gets mixed with mistakes, it patches them and makes things whole. Grace allows you to keep trying, which helps you become better in every way."

13

"She also has my compassionate and nurturing spirit. The compassionate spirit recognizes the tender feelings of others around them, without the person showing physical evidence of those tender feelings sometimes.

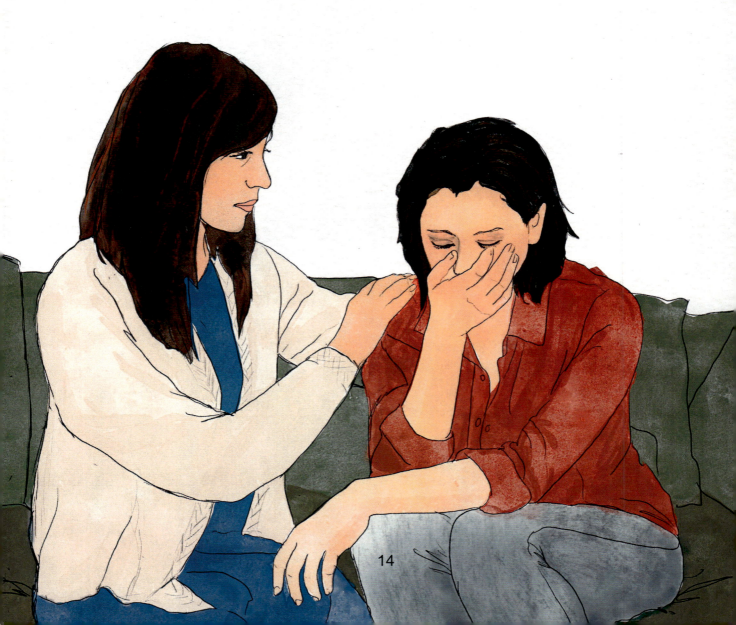

14

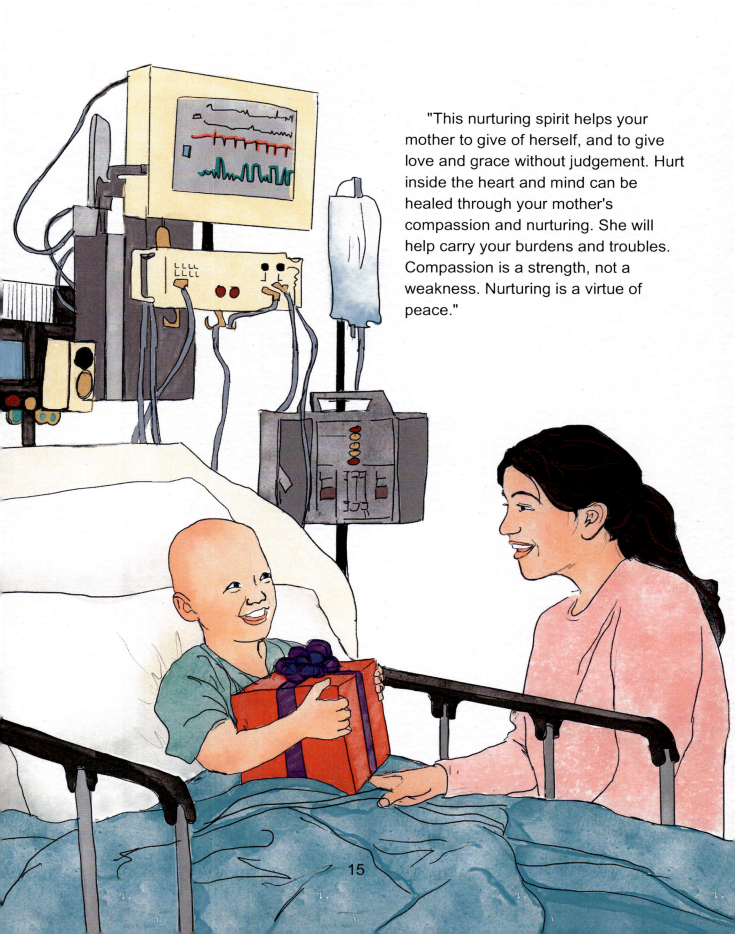

"This nurturing spirit helps your mother to give of herself, and to give love and grace without judgement. Hurt inside the heart and mind can be healed through your mother's compassion and nurturing. She will help carry your burdens and troubles. Compassion is a strength, not a weakness. Nurturing is a virtue of peace."

15

"I created her,
so you will still be able
to feel my love through
her. All women have this gift. It is
called charity. Charity is my pure love,
which is unchallenged and
unquestionable love; it is the most
perfect form of love, joy, and peace.

16

"My love for you and all my children does not quake or shake. Charity is so important that without it, all other gifts I have given to your mother could not function properly."

"Charity is always in your mother's heart and on her mind because it is the most important quality to her. She understands charity so well and clearly that she can give it directly to you from me. This gift ties the family together and never runs out. Charity never fails, nor is it ever forgotten.

18

"Charity can be felt in all my children. You can feel charity from your mother when she holds you, when she kisses you, when you receive a note from her, and even from hearing her sweet voice. Charity is felt powerfully when children reflect gratefully upon their mothers and me."

19

"Remember, I am always with her because of the gifts she has. She will love you the same way I love you.

"I gave your mother all these attributes and blessings. These blessings make your mother the most incredible and unique person that will ever be in your life. Please do not take your mother for granted because she reflects me, and to me, she is perfect for you.

Tyson and Christ turned into another part of his mother's life. She was praying and crying. Tyson knew this was a tender situation. The light of Christ surrounded them. Christ continued softly, sorrowfully, and respectfully, "Sometimes through life she will feel discouraged, inadequate, and alone. She will have difficult times and pain. Help her by honoring her, being with her like you are now, and listen to the Holy Spirit tell you what to do."

GRANDM

22

Tyson listened to the still, small voice. With charity and grief in his heart, he whispered into his mother's ear, "I love you, mother, and you are perfect for me. I am sorry for your loss." He then kissed her on the cheek.

Jesus and Tyson were back in Heaven. Christ wrapped His arms around Tyson. Tyson closed his eyes and felt the warmth of God all around him. He then said lovingly, "Thank you. I am honored to be her child."

Still feeling the warmth of God, he opened his eyes and saw his mother looking into them with the same smile that Jesus had given him moments ago.

Tyson heard the most beautiful voice in the world say, "Your daddy and I love you, Tyson. You are perfect for us."

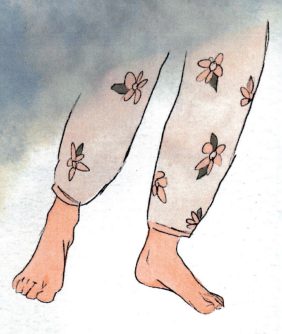

29

Quotes

From General Conference talk "Mother Told Me" (April 2010) by Bradley D. Foster Of the Second Quorum of the Seventy: "Perhaps the reason we respond so universally to our mothers' love is because it typifies the love of the Savior. As President Joseph F. Smith said, 'The love of a true mother comes nearer [to] being like the love of God than any other kind of love' ("The Love of Mother, "Improvement Era. Jan. 1910, 278)."

From General Conference talk "Privileges and Responsibilities of Sisters" (October 1978) by Spencer W. Kimball, President of the Chruch: "Women display a remarkable capacity to love, to cope, along with a remarkable empathy for others in difficulty, which moves women to service as they express their goodness quietly. Women, so often, are Charity personified.

About the Author

Nick DeMann was born and raised in Murray, Utah. After being discouraged at a young age from ever writing a book, Nick was determined to prove that wrong. He took inspiration from the most important women in his life: his mother, Wini, his grandmothers Verna Challis and Elsa DeMann, and his 'Aussie grandma', Nancy Young. Their influence in his life has shaped him into who he is today.

The idea for this book came to be shortly after learning of the death of Nancy. Nick was reflecting gratefully upon his 'Aussie grandma' when he felt words enter into his heart, "She is perfect for you."

In his adult life, Nick was diagnosed with Autism and invites all those who read this book to be more sympathetic to people with developmental, mental and physical challenges. Either way, they are perfect in God's eyes.

Nick lives in Utah with his wife and three sons. He would like to thank everyone who helped this book come to be, especially Mandee Monson, for lending her special talents and making the book come to life, and Josie, his wife, for being by his side every step of the way.

Contact him at nickdemannauthor@gmail.com

Made in United States
North Haven, CT
15 November 2023

44082713R00018